DOORWAY TO MEDITATION

TEXT BY AVERY BROOKE
DRAWINGS BY ROBERT PINART

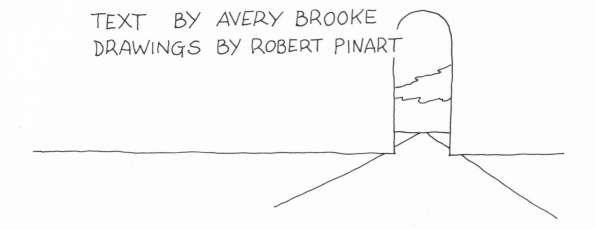

A VINEYARD BOOK

The Seabury Press

New York

1978

The Seabury Press
815 Second Avenue
New York, N.Y. 10017

copyright © 1973 by Vineyard Books, Inc.
First printing 1973, second 1975, third 1978
ISBN : 0-8164-0903-X
Library of Congress card # : 78-51941
Printed in the United States of America

THIS BOOK IS A NARRATIVE ABOUT
JEWS, CHRISTIANS and meditation.
It starts in our common past,
questions many of our present
attitudes and offers a challenge
for the future.

DOORWAY TO MEDITATION

ONCE UPON A TIME

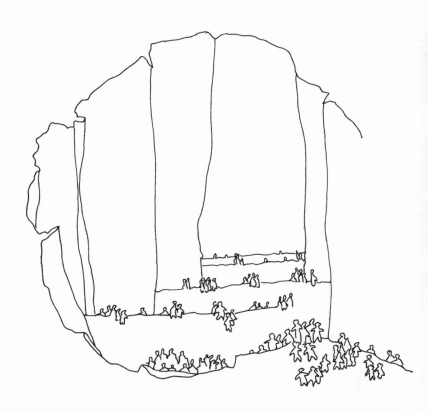

MANY
JEWS and CHRISTIANS
BELIEVED in prayer
AND meditation
AS a WAY OF LIFE.

and some still do,

BUT
today most
of us pray
just once
A WEEK
—IF THAT—
in regular
services
in SYNAGOGUE
or CHURCH.

WHILE A GREAT DEAL OF HINDU
AND Buddhist PRAYER is
DONE ALONE ,

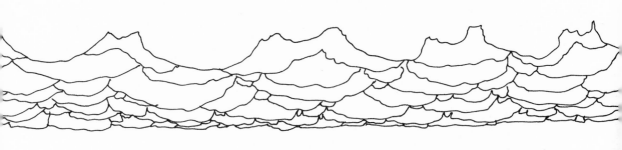

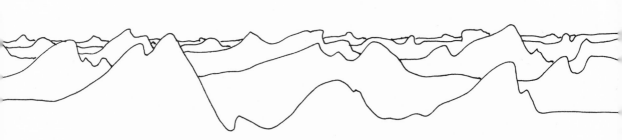

and more frequently.

Ideally, JEWS and CHRISTIANS
BELIEVE in praying
and meditating
ALL the time,

ABOUT
EVERYTHING,

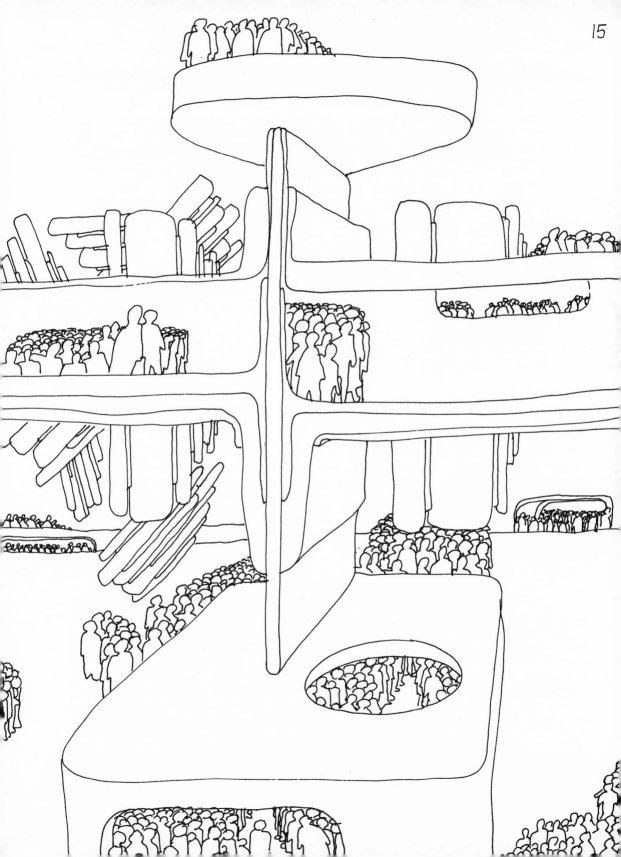

But we Have
Forgotten how.

WE use the
FORMAL PRAYERS
PRAYED BY the GRAND FATHERS
of our great grand fathers,
But
don't KNOW
How
to pray BY
ourselves.

EXCEPT WHEN WE
ARE VERY HAPPY,
OR VERY SAD,
OR VERY AFRAID
THEN it comes naturally,

BUT WE
DON'T
THINK
OF IT
AS PRAYER.

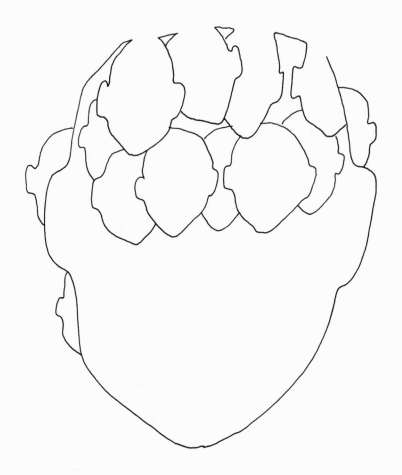

AS FOR MEDITATION
we find it very difficult
to even begin
to say
WHAT IT IS.

surely meditation
is related to prayer,
but then ___

WHAT IS PRAYER?

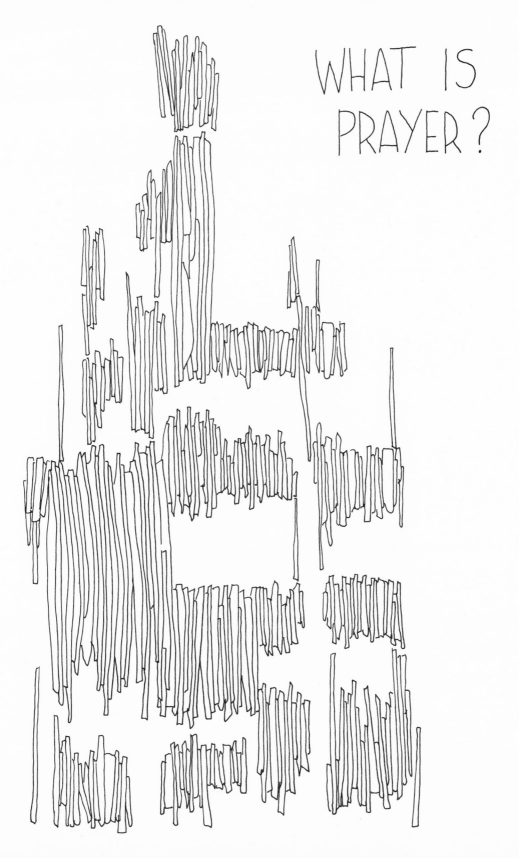

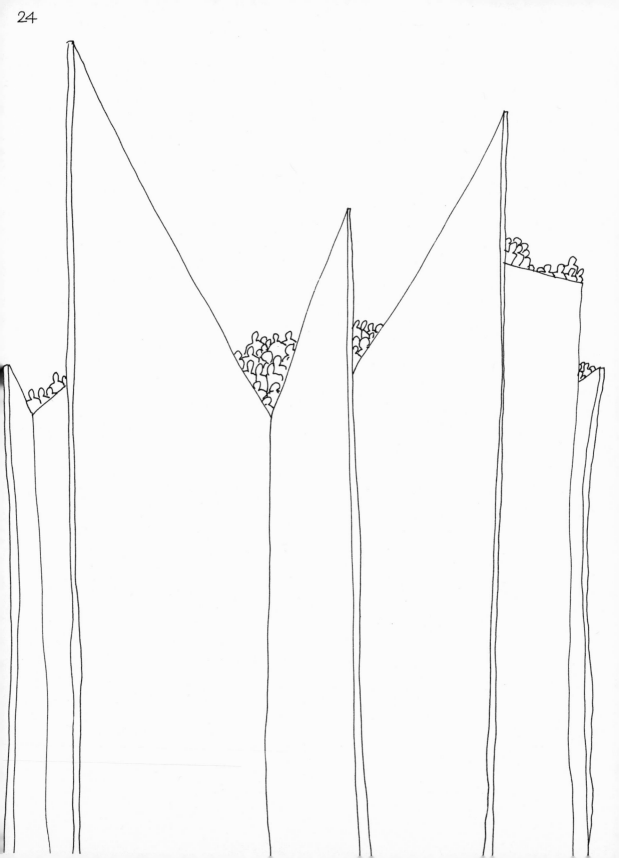

Is it only in the GREAT liturgical and sacramental structure of the ANCIENT FAITHS ?

surely it is also in ____

THE SINGLE
WRENCHED—OUT
WORD :

————————

and THE QUIETER
day by day CONVERSATIONAL
             WORDS
    of THOSE WHO
       FIND HIM
        friend
         and
        master.

or it maybe wordless, imageless.

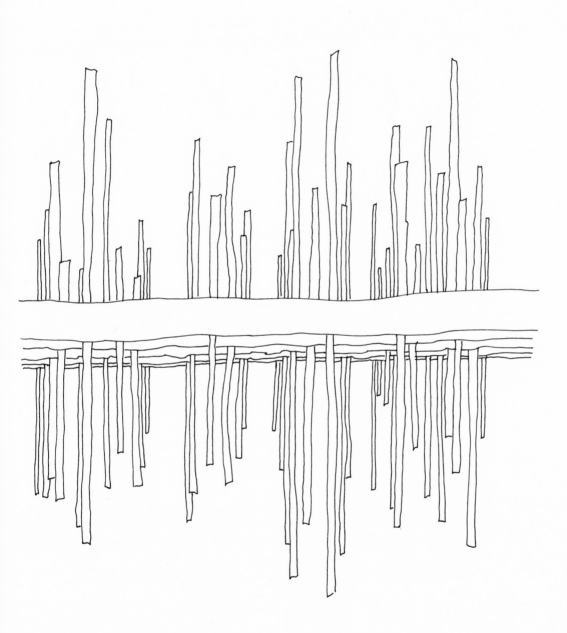

PRAYER is ALSO
EXPRESSED by
Kneeling, BY
PROSTRATING ONESELF
on the floor, by
SACRED DANCE, and
by the VERY ACT of
   SITTING QUIETLY,
with LEGS CROSSED,
      OR BOWING ONE'S
      HEAD,
   OR STANDING IN
      ADORATION
   with head and arms
      RAISED.

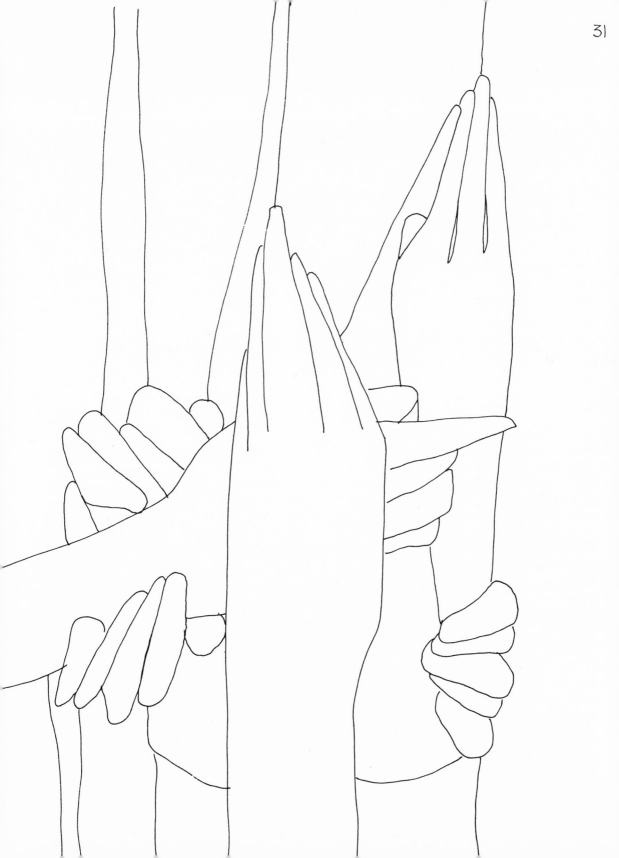

PRAYER MAY BE EXPRESSED
BY FASTING OR BY FEASTING,
BY WORK, BY CHARITY,

OR BY
POLITICS.

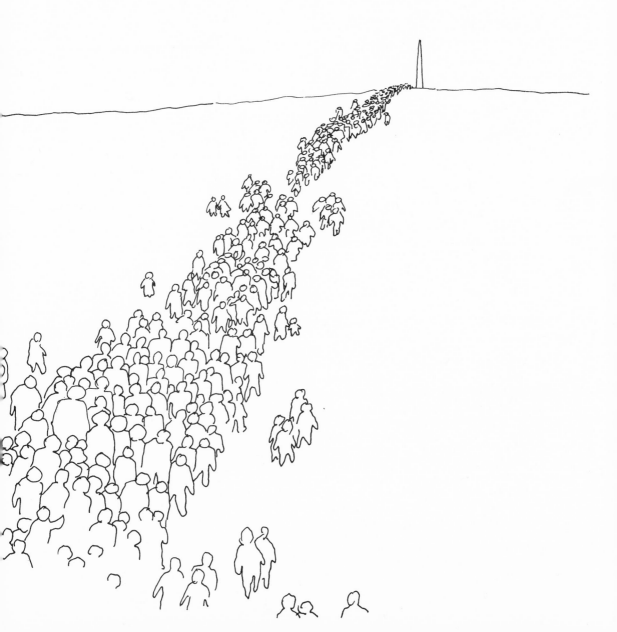

ONE CAN GO FURTHER AND SAY
that painting and poetry
maybe called
PRAYER,
that a useful life is a form
of prayer, THAT SUFFERING
ACCEPTED PATIENTLY is
prayer,
THAT ALL EARTHLY JOYS
accepted
with thanksgiving
ARE PRAYER,
and all
earthly joys
DENIED
FOR GOD'S SAKE
are
prayer.

It appears then, that there is
little that is not sometimes
called prayer, with the exception
of greed and cruelty,
and since the world is
a confusing place,
even they
are
called
prayer from time
to time

BUT
TO BE LEFT
WITH EVERYTHING
LEAVES US
WITH
NOTHING.

PRAYER may take many — an
almost limitless NUMBER
of FORMS,
YET prayers said in
CHURCH or SYNAGOGUE
are often empty.
EMPTY FORMS,
meaningless ritual.
The SAME, however is true
of ALL FORMS of prayer.
To KNEEL is — of itself —
not prayer.
To sit, crossed legged,
for SILENT HOURS
is — of itself — NOT PRAYER.

NEITHER fasting nor
enjoying the pleasures of LIFE
in themselves, ARE PRAYER.
BUT it is EQUALLY true
that IMPROVING personal
RELATIONSHIPS, working
in the GHETTO or REFORMING
political INSTITUTIONS
ARE NOT NECESSARILY
prayer___
         although they may be.

42

the QUESTION
NARROWS DOWN
TO: what is
missing
WHEN
a form of
PRAYER,
IS
EMPTY?

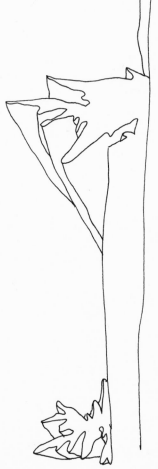

We really know the answer.
We are usually just too
busy to think about it.

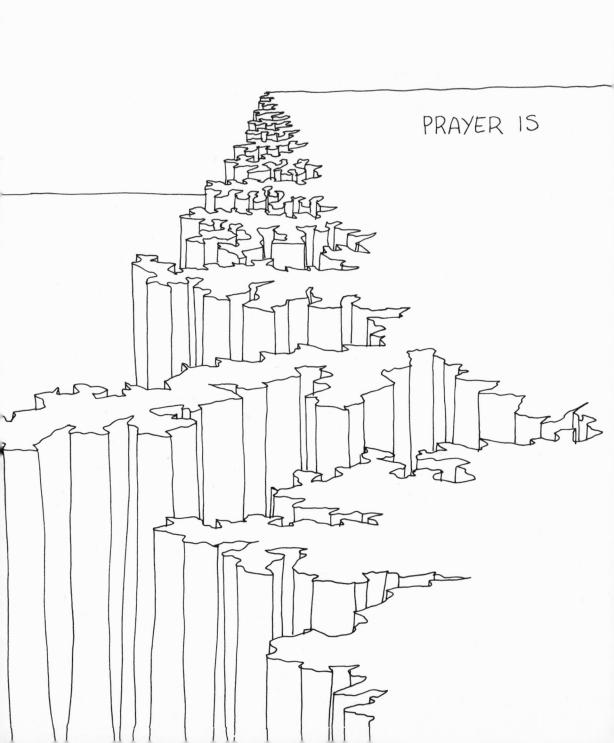

PRAYER IS

A BOND OR COMMUNICATION
BETWEEN
MAN AND
GOD.

WHEN OUR PRAYER
is EMPTY,
it is because
we do not
expect GOD
to reply.

MEDITATION
is
Listening

prayer.

IN a sense,
MEDITATION
may take
ALL the forms
that prayer takes,

FOR GOD may speak to us, even
as WE ARE SPEAKING TO HIM.

AS we PRAISE HIM,
as WE SAY
HIS NAME, as we think
of Him,
as WE speak to HIM,
HIS thoughts come BACK
to us,

and if
we are LISTENING,
we hear them.

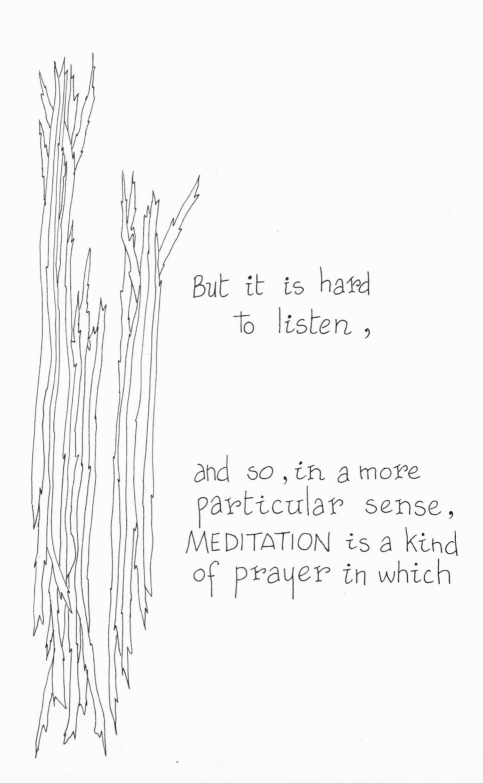

But it is hard
to listen,

and so, in a more
particular sense,
MEDITATION is a kind
of prayer in which

to practice
the art
of LISTENING.

FOR SOME people
and at some times,
speaking to God
AND HEARING HIM,
comes naturally.

for most
people,
most of the time,
it DOES NOT.

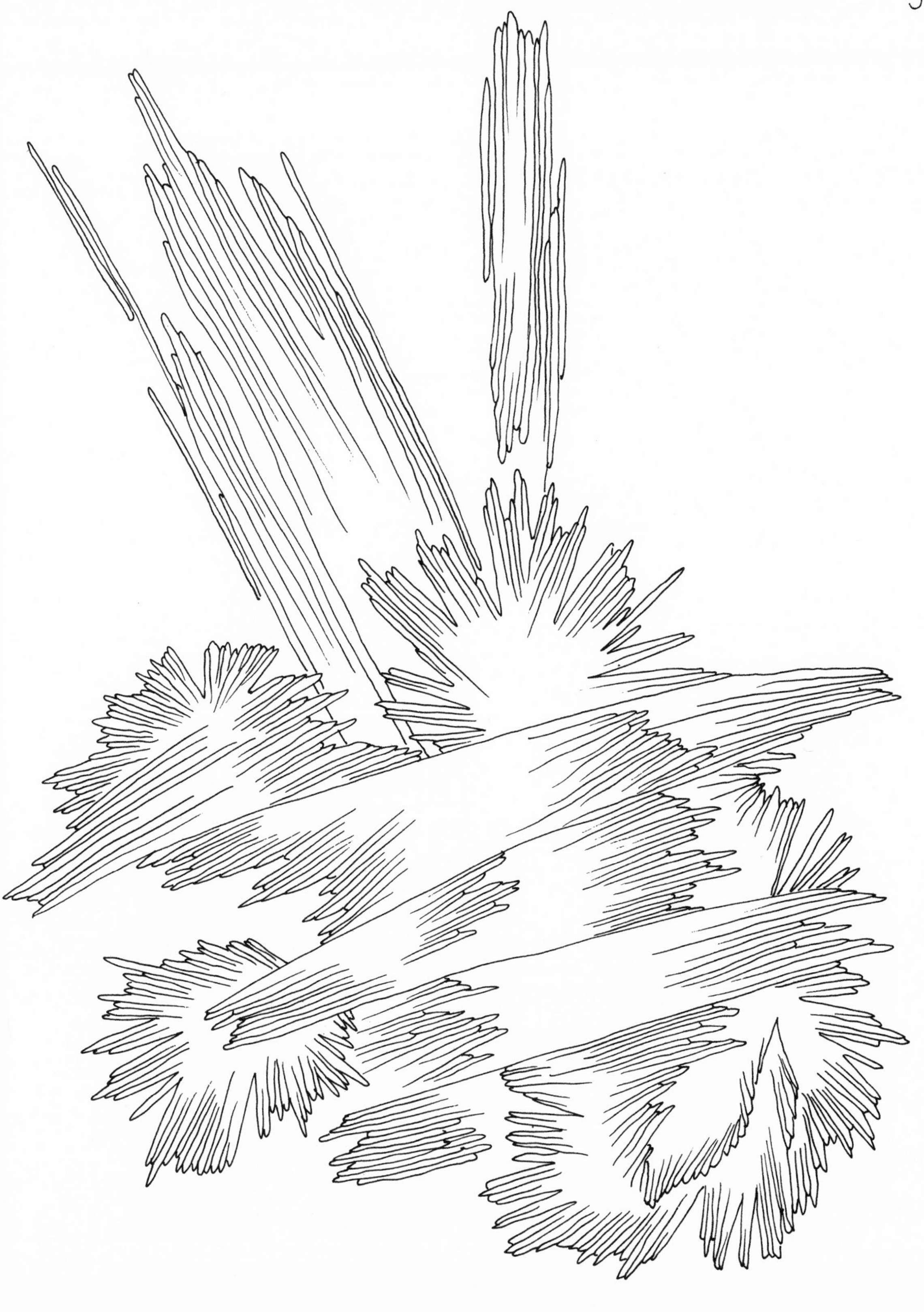

for we are out of
practice.

We've always had
'more important' things
to do.

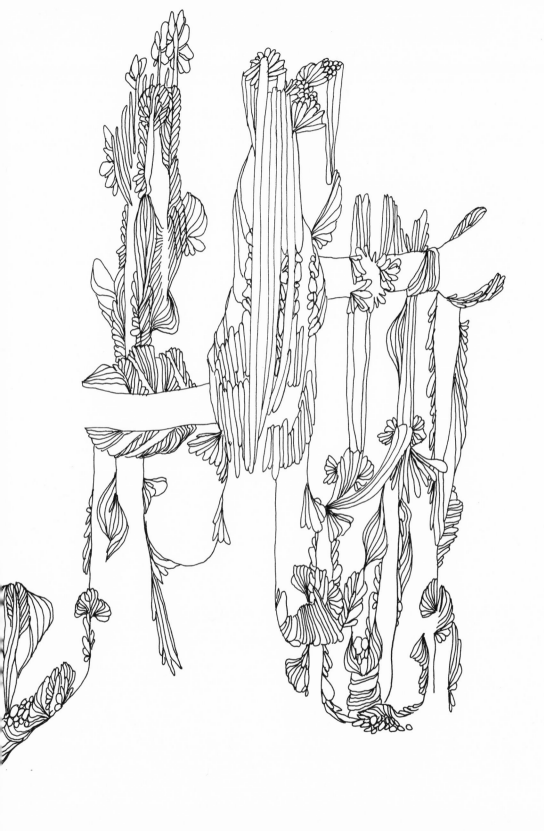

Perhaps this is
because we are afraid
of what we might hear if
WE STOPPED TO LISTEN,

for even in the secular
sense, whether MEDITATION
is relaxed daydreaming
or disciplined and creative
thinking ,

It is an INVITATION to the NEW. _____

LISTENING PRAYER is prayer
in which we are willing to
have GOD write the agenda.

AND THIS TAKES COURAGE

AND WORK.

OUR TRADITION IS CLEAR
ENOUGH:

"You shall
love the Lord your God
with all your heart, and
with all your soul, and with
all your strength."

To LOVE GOD,
You must
KNOW Him and to know Him,
You must
PRAY.

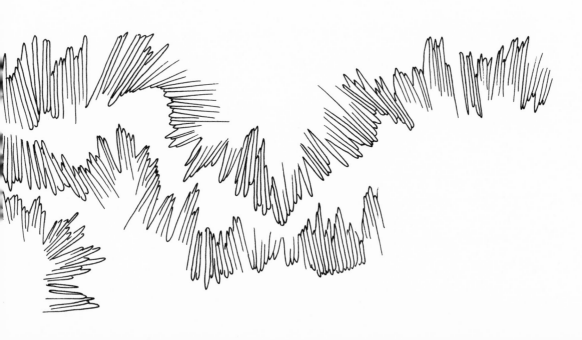

"Seek and ye shall find,
knock and it shall be
opened unto you."

But no CASUAL SEEKING WILL DO,
NO timid KNOCKING on doors
—and then running away
WHEN THEY OPEN A CRACK.

GOD IS HEARD
BY THOSE WHO
KEEP LISTENING.

It is that simple,

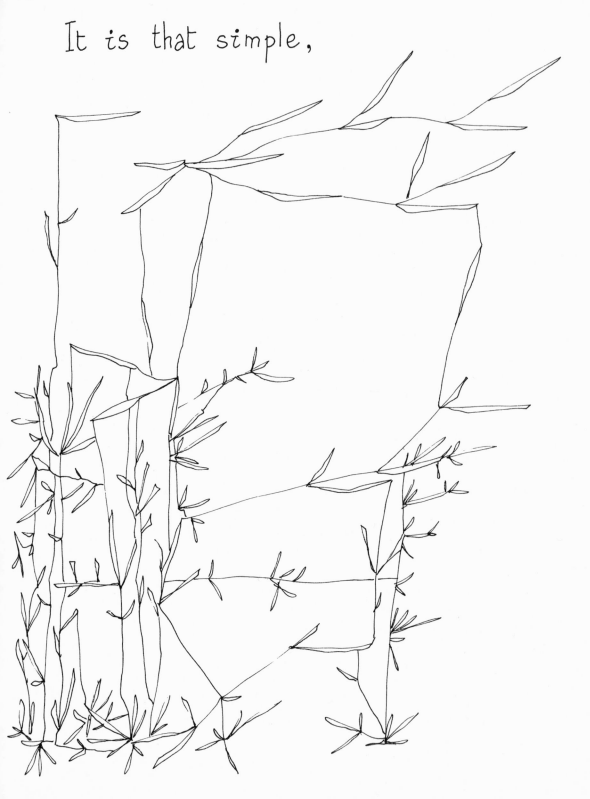

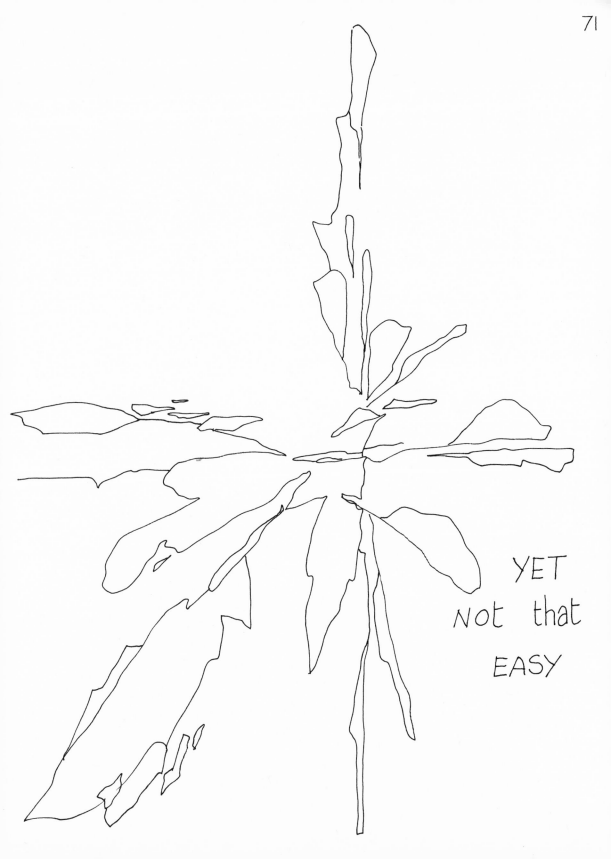

YET
Not that
EASY

THE TROUBLE IS

THAT WE
HAVE
VERY LITTLE
FAITH.

we may
SPEAK
to God

WHEN WE ARE NOT SURE
THAT HE EXISTS

76

BUT how CAN we HEAR HIM?

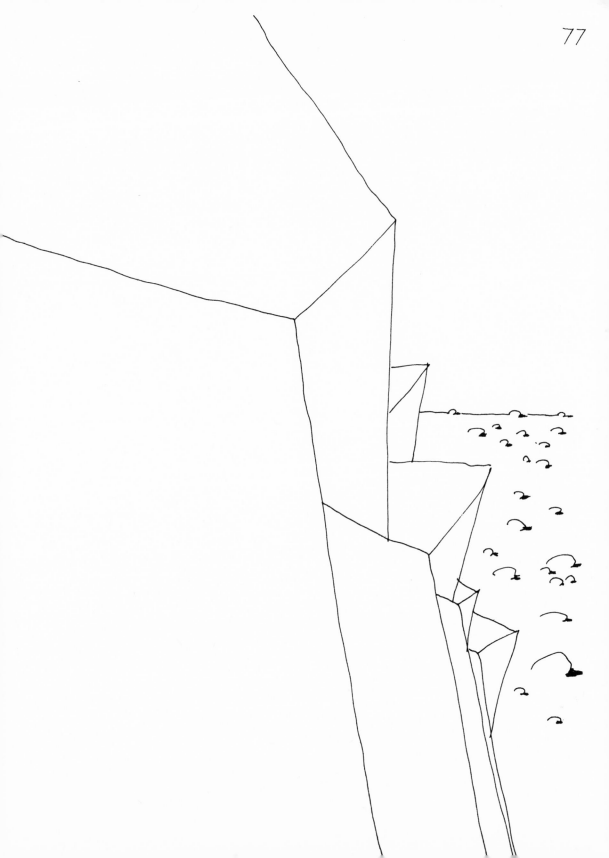

IF GOD spoke to ONE
OF us RIGHT NOW —
IN A VOICE of THUNDER
— the CHANCES ARE
THAT WE WOULD
DECIDE THAT WE
WERE CRAZY.

WE were BROUGHT UP to BELIEVE
IN SOLID FACTS, put TOGETHER
BY the RULES OF REASON. IN
A LITTLE while, SO WE WERE
TAUGHT, MAN would have
everyTHING UNDER
CONTROL.

AND EVEN THOUGH
WE NOW KNOW
THIS IS NOT TRUE,
WE WOULD STILL
LIKE TO HAVE
GOD'S
EXISTENCE PROVED
TO US —

OR DISPROVED.

OBLIGINGLY, SCHOLARS hAVE
SUBJECTED the BiBLE and
THEOLOGY to THE MOST MICRO-
SCOPIC AND CRITICAL ANALYSIS.
WE NOW KNOW A LOT MORE
THAN OUR GRANDFATHERS Knew
about the CITIES OF
ANCIENT ISRAEL, about
who WROTE WHAT, AND
WHO saiD what — OR DIDN'T
—AND why.
THE LETTERS of St. Paul
have been put THROUGH
a COMPUTER and ruins
of HOLY places have been carbon
tested. EVERY word of MOSES, the

PRophets, Jesus and the Disciples
have been ANALYZED IN THE LIGHT
of HISTORY, Philosophy, Psychology,
Sociology , LINGUISTICS
AND special sciences[1]
INVENTED for THE PURPOSE.[2]

1. With footnotes
2. The next book contradicts and
   dissects further. And has
   footnotes on the earlier book.

BUT NO
MATTER HOW
GREAT THE
SCHOLARSHIP

MAN MAY NOT CATCH
  GOD IN A NET
AND PEER AT
  HIM THROUGH A
MICROSCOPE ,

Scholarship, THOUGH OFTEN
SUPPORTIVE,
ILLUMINATING
AND INSPIRING,

DOES NOT
GIVE US
FAITH.

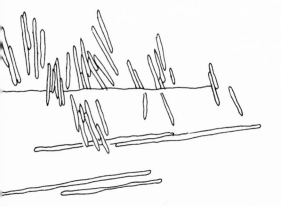

WE
GET MAD
AT RELIGION.

WE
THINK THAT
IT SHOULD
BE PROVIDING
US
WITH THE ONE
GREAT
CERTAINTY
AND INSTEAD
IT SEEMS
TO BE
PRAISING
UNCERTAINTY .

THE GROUND SHIFTS BENEATH OUR FEET AND WE TRY DESPERATELY TO HOLD ONTO OLD CERTAINTIES OR TO FIND NEW ONES.

WE THINK
OF AN AGE
OF FAITH
AS AN AGE OF CERTITUDE ,

YET HAVING FAITH
DOES NOT
MEAN
KNOWING
CERTAINLY.

NOR DOES
IT
MEAN
THAT WE
HAVE
TO SIT
AROUND
AND WAIT
FOR A
BLINDING
CONVERSION,

OR politely go through
the FORMS,
'just in case'.

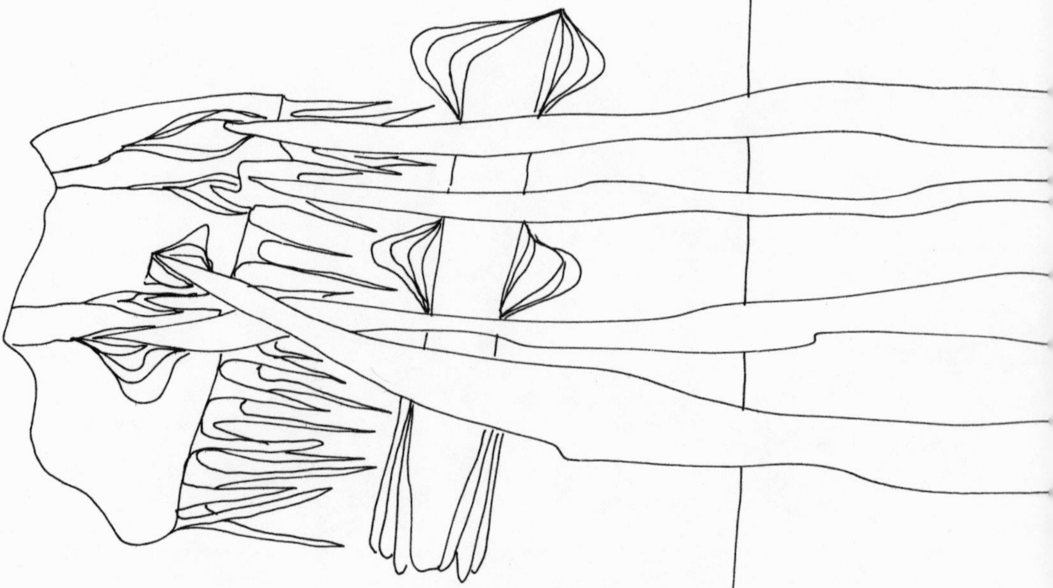

IT JUST MEANS
that we must
stop WORRYING SO MUCH ABOUT
WHAT WE DON'T BELIEVE and LEARN
to LISTEN for WHISPERS
of the unprovable
INFINITE.

FAITH BEGINS WITH KNOWLEDGE OF GOD

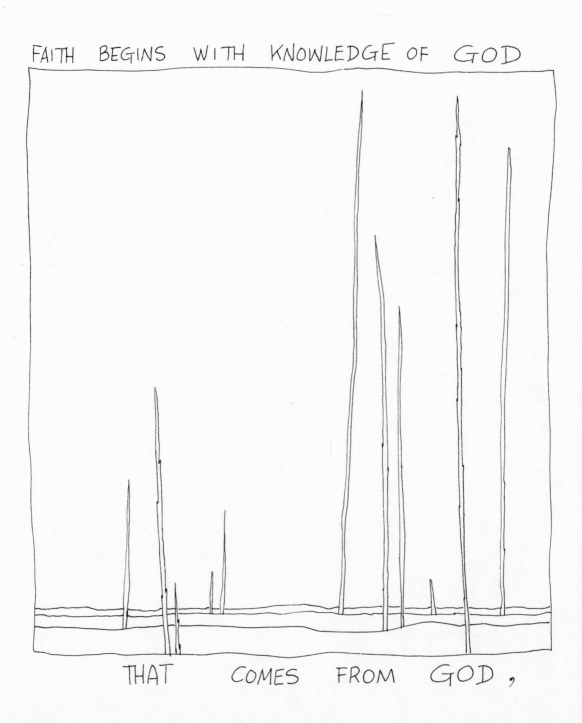

THAT COMES FROM GOD ,

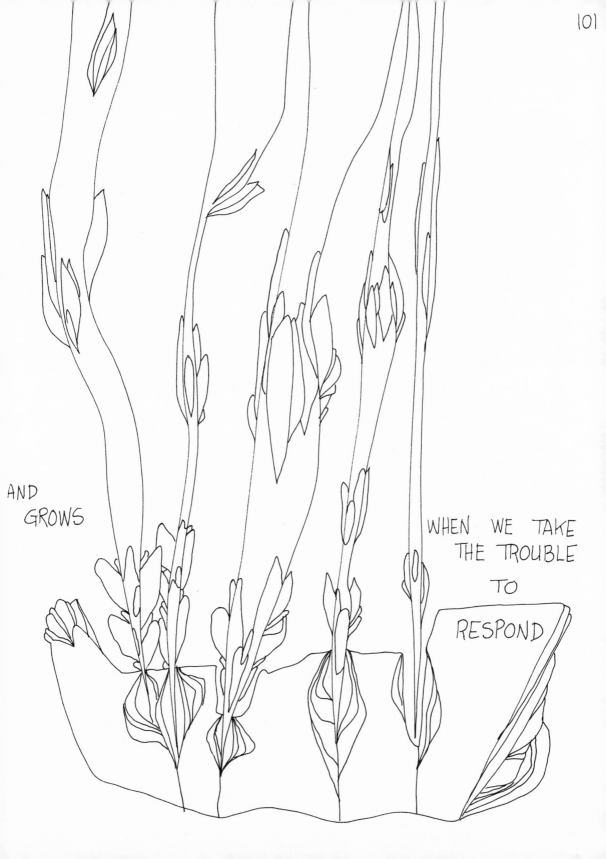

AND
GROWS

WHEN WE TAKE
THE TROUBLE
TO
RESPOND

FAITH IS
A DIRECTION,
NOT AN END.

IT is A JOURNEY TOWARDS GOD,
NOT GOD HIMSELF.

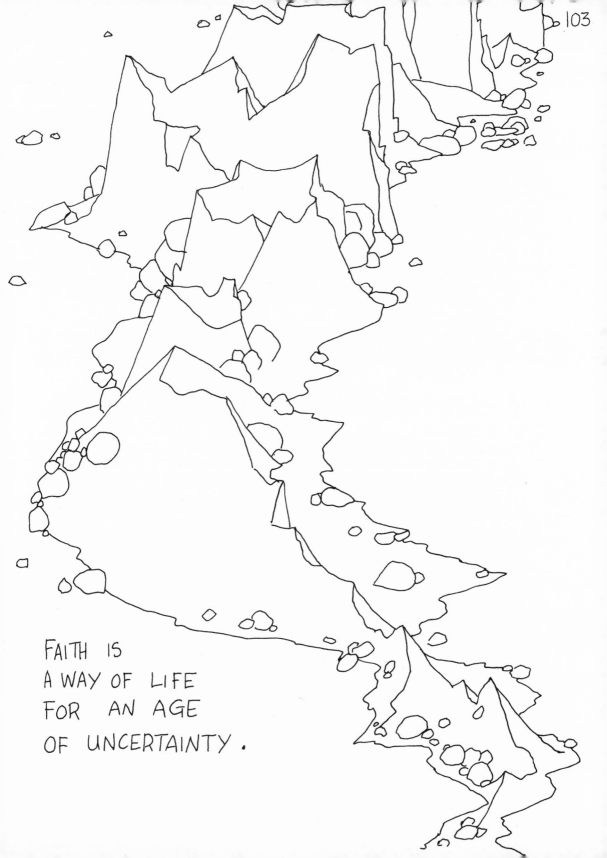

FAITH IS
A WAY OF LIFE
FOR AN AGE
OF UNCERTAINTY.

IN our minds
and HEARTS, in
the happenings
of each day,
IN THE HILLS

and in the
streets,
in horror
and happiness

GOD
IS THERE

and if we listen,
and do not turn away,
we will hear Him.

FAITH ACCEPTS THE
POSSIBILITY THAT
GOD
MAY HAVE SOMETHING
TO SAY TO US,
AS WELL AS
WE TO HIM.

This is the doorway
to meditation.

POSTSCRIPT

The foregoing pages are
an attempt to open a door
to another country. Except
perhaps vicariously, they
do not take you into that
country and they say very
little about how to get there.
If you now feel that you
would like to go through
that door, and that there
is indeed a country
beyond it, then they have
accomplished their purpose.

But the question remains:
why have I and my friend,
Robert Pinart, produced
a book that only takes you
to the threshold? Because
I believe that these two
initial steps, that of seeing
and that of desiring, are so

vital, that to present them as part of a "how to do it" book, would be to lessen their impact.

I am now working on a very practical manuscript concerning how to learn, practice and teach the kind of meditation described in this book. In a sense, it will be a sequel, but necessarily very different in form and content. This does not mean that you should wait before crossing the threshold. It is the Spirit of God who is the teacher. Men are but His instruments, and methods are only our imperfect supports and guideposts.

Trust Him. Ask Him where
you should begin. And
start to listen.

A. B.

Noroton, Connecticut, 1973

This sequel has now
been finished. It is en-
titled How TO MEDITATE
WITHOUT LEAVING THE
WORLD. (1975)

Since then I have also
written HIDDEN IN PLAIN
SIGHT: The Practice of
Christian Meditation. (1978)